The 1980s

John Peacock

Fashion Sourcebooks The 1980s

With 317 illustrations

Thames and Hudson

For Jenny Shircore

© 1998 Thames and Hudson Ltd,
London

British Library Cataloguing-
in-Publication Data
A catalogue record for this book is
available from the British Library.

ISBN 0-500-28076-2

Printed and bound in Slovenia by
Mladinska Knjiga

Contents

In the 1980s, youth culture no longer dominated fashion. In male dress, the peacock look of the seventies gave way to a more sophisticated, formal elegance. Men wanted clothes that were both business-like and comfortable, as well as being of a recognizably high quality in a decade that was greatly concerned with status. A typical outfit for men consisted of a double-breasted jacket worn with straight-cut trousers with pleats from the waist. For smart occasions, a designer-label jacket was often combined with blue denim jeans and an open-necked silk shirt.

Clothes by top designers were a leitmotif of the eighties. Department stores were rearranged to cater for a new way of merchandising, with in-house designer boutiques selling everything from coats and suits to accessories and perfumes – all under one designer label.

For women as well as men, minimal elegance was the aim. The 'executive look', which had first found expression as part of working women's dress in the 1970s, matured into what became known as 'power dressing'. This style was based on the male silhouette, and was achieved through a skirt suit which combined a wide, shoulder-padded jacket with a feminizing short skirt. The jacket hung from the shoulders, skimming the waist and disguising the hips. It was a strong, aggressive silhouette. Trouser suits, though still worn, were less in evidence than they had been in the seventies.

Glamour was reserved for the evening. In the early part of the decade, ball gowns in silk and satin with huge skirts and outsized bows and frills were much in vogue (wedding dresses were similarly styled). In the later eighties these rather fairytale garments gave way to overtly body-conscious styles such as mini-length, skimpy dresses in Lycra or leather, with strapless boned bodices reminiscent of corsets. Azzedine Alaïa, Gianni

Versace and Thierry Mugler were among a number of designers who contributed provocative, body-hugging garments to the female wardrobe.

Many designers favoured natural materials, including silk, wool, cotton and linen. The Italians, in particular Giorgio Armani, were responsible for a vogue for softly tailored crumpled linens, and this fabric achieved widespread popularity. Trousers and jackets in linen or cotton became fashionable leisure wear for men.

Young Japanese designers produced avant-garde collections of oversized, often asymmetric clothes, predominantly in black, ink-blue and black-brown. These were often slashed and creased, with irregularly placed necklines, collars and sleeves.

Some fabrics were mixtures of new and old: polyester with cotton, for example, or Lycra with wool. Polyamides, rayon and nylon were also used together. The mixed fabrics took dyes well, giving rise to bright colours and jazzy printed patterns which were used for leisure wear and beach wear. Leisure and sports wear had by this time merged with casual wear. Tracksuits became familiar on the street, while white trainers and baseball caps found particular favour with the young.

Accessories for both men and women were refined and of high quality. Men chose classic shoes for business wear, and for leisure use coloured deck shoes in canvas, suede or leather were popular.

Women's shoes ranged from slingbacks with medium-high, slender heels to mannish designs with laces or buckles and straps. Also popular were knee-high boots with either high spiked heels or low, stacked cuban heels. Black or dark stockings or tights were especially favoured as skirts grew shorter later in the decade.The most popular bags were shoulder bags with long, adjustable straps and quilted leather bags with chain handles.

Hats were reserved for occasions such as races and weddings. Women's special-occasion hats tended to be shallow-crowned with wide brims. Men rarely wore hats at all, apart from top hats at weddings, though caps were still common at country sporting occasions.

As is usually the case, men's fashions in this decade developed more slowly than women's, so they have been shown on average with one example per page.

In the main, the fashions I have used are such as would have been worn by men and women of the middle or upper-middle classes and by people who, while not necessarily being 'dedicated followers of fashion', would have had a keen interest in the latest styles. The sources from which I have drawn – chiefly from Great Britain, North America, France and Italy – include contemporary magazines, catalogues and journals; museum collections; original dated photographs and my own costume collection. This Sourcebook is divided into ten sections, each of which includes four subdivisions covering Day Wear, Evening Wear (alternately on two occasions, Wedding Wear), Sports and Leisure Wear and a section on either Underwear or Accessories. Following the main illustrations are ten pages of schematic drawings accompanied by detailed notes about each example, giving particulars of colour, fabric, cut and trimming as well as accessories and other useful information.

Then follow two pages of drawings which illustrate the decade 'at a glance' and which demonstrate the evolution of the period and its main development trends.

Biographies of the most important international fashion designers of the decade are also included as well as a list of further reading suggestions into the styles of this period.

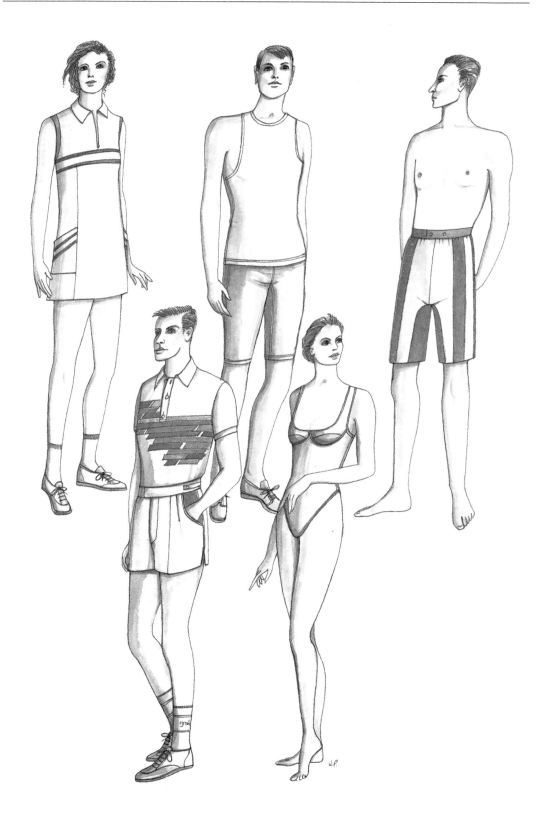

1980 Day Wear

1 Navy-blue crepe-de-chine dress, bloused bodice and below-knee-length skirt cut without waist seam, gathered in on waist by navy-blue leather buckled belt, padded shoulders, full-length inset sleeves, white crepe-de-chine frilled cuffs gathered under cherry-red ribbon bands, matching collar and bow-tie. Navy-blue leather shoes, almond-shaped toes, high stacked heels. 2 Light-brown rayon dress, random pattern of black spots, unfitted bodice and knee-length skirt cut without waist seam, knife-pleats from under shaped yoke, padded shoulders, full-length inset sleeves, button trim above hem, white top-stitched collar, brown petersham ribbon bow-tie. Brown patent-leather sling-back shoes, round toes, bow trim, thick medium-high heels. 3 Pink, yellow and green knitted-wool sweater dress, all-over geometric patterns, mini-length skirt, ribbed hemline, deep yoke, high round neckline, padded shoulders, long cuffed inset sleeves, dropped shoulderline. Pink and green striped knitted-wool tights. Green leather step-in shoes, round toes, flat heels. 4 Dark-brown wool-tweed jacket, single-breasted fastening, flap pockets. Light-brown wool tapered trousers, pleats from waist, no turn-ups. Burgundy and beige Argyle check lambswool sweater, V-shaped neckline. Pale-blue wool collar-attached shirt worn over light-brown knitted-wool polo-neck sweater. Pale-blue scarf, fringed hems. Brown leather step-in shoes. 5 Dark mustard-yellow leather two-piece suit: wrapover hip-length jacket, self-fabric tie belt, wide lapels, brown fur collar, matching cuffs on full-length inset sleeves, padded shoulders, hip-level pockets set into vertical panel seams; knee-length straight skirt, seamed on low hip-level, top-stitched edges and detail. Cream silk T-shirt. Brown leather shoes.

Evening Wear

1 Navy-blue wool two-piece evening suit: edge-to-edge jacket, fastening with linked buttons, long shawl collar faced with blue silk, piped pockets; tapered trousers, no turn-ups. White cotton collar-attached shirt, concealed fastening, top-stitched edges, navy-blue silk bow-tie. Black leather lace-up shoes. 2 Black sequined evening dress, semi-fitted bodice, narrow ankle-length skirt, back vent to knee-level, deep V-shaped neckline, padded shoulders, full-length inset sleeves. Black satin shoes, pointed toes. 3 Pleated polyester-crepe evening dress, asymmetric upper bodice draped from one shoulder in lilac, draped asymmetric midriff and bow-knot detail in yellow, ankle-length skirt in bright-pink. Pink suede strap sandals. 4 Royal-blue polyester-crepe three-piece evening suit: short edge-to-edge jacket, small collar worn turned up, padded shoulders, full-length inset sleeves, top-stitched edges; chemise top gathered from straight neckline, narrow shoestring straps; ankle-length drainpipe trousers split on outside seams above hems, gathers from waist, side-hip pockets, pink polyester satin belt. Royal-blue satin strap sandals, high spike heels. 5 Sleeveless cream satin ballgown, woven pattern of silver and gold butterflies, bloused bodice, full-length gathered skirt worn over stiffened petticoats, off-the-shoulder neckline edged with deep frill of cream silk organdie, woven pattern of silver and gold butterflies and scattered with silver and gold sequins, matching gathered scalloped frill above hemline, large organdie bow trim on one side of neckline.

Sports and Leisure Wear

1 Cricket. Handknitted cream cotton sweater, low V-shaped neckline edged in blue and green, matching bands above ribbed cuffs of full-length inset sleeves. Cream wool-flannel tapered trousers, hip-level pockets, no turn-ups. Cream brushed-cotton collar-attached shirt. Green wool peaked cap, blue trim. Cream leather lace-up spiked cricket boots. 2 Ski wear. Sleeveless red wool jacket, zip fastening to under high stand collar; red, blue, purple and yellow geometric-patterned yoke, matching lining, hip-level welt pockets, button trim. Red wool sweater, high round neckline, full-length cuffed sleeves. Wool and nylon ski pants. Brimless red knitted-wool hat, matching jacket pattern. 3 Casual wear. Dark-yellow leather jacket, zip fastening to under large collar, stitched and tucked yoke, full-length sleeves, chest-level zipped pockets, matching vertical pockets above hemline. Dark-brown cotton tapered trousers, knee-level seam, inset zipped pocket, side-hip pockets, no creases or turn-ups. Burnt-orange knitted-wool sweater, V-shaped neckline, full-length sleeves. Cream cotton collar-attached shirt. White canvas trainers, yellow trim. 4 Casual wear. Turquoise brushed-cotton all-in-one jumpsuit, zip fastening from hip-level to under stand collar, full-length shirt-style sleeves, inset elasticated half-belt, button trim, matching low hip-level pockets, tapered legs. Sleeveless turquoise cotton jacket, multicoloured printed pattern, zip fastening under large collar, zipped side-hip pockets, elasticated hipband. Long tan leather boots, flat heels. 5 Holiday wear. Yellow cotton dress, white seagull print, yoke bodice, gathered halter straps, three-tier skirt, central panel white with red seagulls, matching yellow and white print stole. Striped cotton shoes, rope soles.

Underwear and Negligee

1 White rayon-satin nightdress, ankle-length skirt gathered from under shaped cups, wide V-shaped neckline formed by two wide-set embroidered-velvet ribbon shoulder straps infilled with fine rayon-lace. 2 Pale-peach Lycra-satin soft cup bra, lace trim, front fastening, adjustable shoulder straps, hip-level bikini briefs in matching fabric, rayon-lace side panels, high-cut legs. 3 Black silk one-piece camisole and French knickers, low shaped neckline edged with black scalloped lace to match side edges of high-cut legs, narrow self-fabric shoulder straps, crotch fastening. 4 Primrose-yellow Lycra-satin bra, low scooped neckline forming half-cups, scalloped lace infill, back fastening, low-cut bikini briefs in matching fabric, top edge trimmed with scalloped lace, high-cut legs. 5 Wine-red panne-velvet dressing gown, wrapover bloused bodice, roll collar, scalloped edge embroidered with self-colour flowers and leaves, padded shoulders, bishop-style inset sleeves gathered into rouleau cuffs, matching tie-belt, ankle-length gathered skirts. 6 Dark-blue wool dressing gown, front edges and roll collar piped in red to match ends of self-fabric tie-belt, mock cuffs of full-length inset sleeves and top edges of patch pockets, breast pocket with embroidered monogram. Red cotton pyjamas. Red leather step-in slippers.

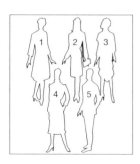

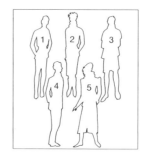

1981 Day Wear

1 Sage-green wool dress, knee-length skirt flared from high waist position, unpressed pleats from side-front panel seams in upper bodice, high round neckline, deep slash on centre front, padded shoulders, three-quarter-length flared inset sleeves, hems trimmed with black braid, matching skirt hem, top-stitched edges and detail. Black suede shoes, black patent-leather toecaps and high spike heels.
2 Bright-red acetate and nylon two-piece suit, spotted in dark-red, black and white: single-breasted unfitted hip-length jacket, white peter-pan collar, gathered shaping from under yoke seam, padded shoulders, full-length inset sleeves gathered into narrow cuffs, self-fabric belt and covered buckle; knee-length gathered skirt. Small black felt hat, low crown, red plastic band, narrow brim. Black leather shoulder bag; matching shoes, peep toes.
3 Black knitted-wool sweater dress, outsized polo-neck collar, full-length sleeves, ribbed cuffs, straight knee-length skirt. Charcoal-grey wool-flannel wrap, bias-cut, single armhole, worn draped over one shoulder. Black leather shoes, almond-shaped toes, high heels.
4 Coffee-coloured silk dress spotted in brown, bloused bodice buttoned from waist to under frilled neckline, matching edge of square yoke and hemline of knee-length skirt, padded shoulders, full-length inset sleeves gathered into cuffs, self-fabric tie-belt, hip-level pockets set into side seams. Dark-brown leather sling-back shoes, peep toes, high spike heels. 5 Dark-cream linen jacket flecked with black and brown, single-breasted two-button fastening, narrow lapels, patch pockets, side vents. Black linen tapered trousers, no turn-ups. Cream linen collar-attached shirt. Pink silk tie, black and brown pattern. Black lace-up shoes, perforated detail.

Evening Wear

1 Turquoise satin two-piece evening ensemble: edge-to-edge bolero jacket, outsized collar faced with pintucked grey silk, matching cuffs of full-length bishop sleeves, appliqué of pink and green waterlilies on hem of sleeves, matching hemline of ground-length gathered skirt of dress, fitted strapless bodice, pintucked decoration from central seam. 2 Primrose-yellow silk-taffeta ballgown, fitted and boned bodice, waistline with centre-front point, off-the-shoulder neckline edged with wide frill, central bow trim, matching detail above two-tier frill on hem of elbow-length outsized puffed sleeves, ground-length gathered skirt worn over stiffened petticoats. 3 Gold lamé evening dress, bloused bodice, horizontal tucks forming yoke above bustline, matching detail above hemline of ankle-length gathered skirt, high neckline, padded shoulders, elbow-length sleeves gathered on shoulders and into narrow cuffs on hem, self-fabric tie-belt. Gold kid strap sandals. 4 Black silk-taffeta evening gown, fitted and boned bodice, off-the-shoulder neckline caught up to centre-front neck by self-fabric rouleau band, edge of neckline trimmed with narrow frill to match hemline of ground-length gathered skirt and trim on edge of draped black satin belt, full-length sleeves. 5 White silk-jersey evening dress, low neckline, self-fabric rouleau straps, semi-fitted bodice and ankle-length skirt cut without waist seam; white, silver and crystal bead embroidery from under neckline to knee-level, bunches of white ostrich feathers trim from knee-level to hemline. White satin shoes, pointed toes.

Sports and Leisure Wear

1 Tennis. White knitted-cotton shirt striped in yellow and blue, V-shaped neckline, plain-blue collar matching cuffs of short inset sleeves. White cotton shorts, side-hip pockets. White canvas trainers, white cotton ankle socks. 2 Casual wear. Light-brown leather collarless jacket, fitted upper bodice, horizontal tucks above self-fabric belt to bust-level, asymmetric fastening, padded shoulders, stitched epaulettes, full-length sleeves, stitched cuffs, pockets set into diagonal seams of skirt, top-stitched edges and detail. Brown velvet breeches, knee-level cuffs. Brown wool sweater, outsized polo-neck collar, long sleeves, matching tights. Long brown leather boots, decorative ruching above ankles, almond-shaped toes. 3 Holiday wear. Pale-green two-piece safari suit: unfitted hip-length jacket, single-breasted fastening with press-studs, shirt collar, shaped yoke, epaulettes, button trim; bermuda-length shorts, turn-ups, dark-green leather belt. White cotton T-shirt. Dark-green leather T-strap sandals, openwork detail, crepe soles. 4 Ski wear. Pink rayon and wool mixture two-piece ski suit: jacket zip fastening from hem to under dark-blue collar, matching yoke and upper part of full-length inset sleeves, elasticated inset waistband, hip-level zipped pockets, top-stitched edges and detail; mid-calf-length trousers, elasticated hems. Ski boots. Blue and pink knitted-wool hat worn over pink wool cowl. White ski boots, dark-blue trim. 5 Country wear. Dark-cream cotton-velvet cord jacket, single-breasted fastening, brown suede yoke, padded shoulders, full-length sleeves, gathered on shoulders, flap pockets. Cream, brown and red checked wool mid-calf-length culottes, off-centre knife-pleats, hip-level pockets. Brick-red wool polo-neck sweater flecked with brown. Brown leather pumps.

Accessories

1 White straw hat, wide brim, outsized sunglasses. 2 Dark-brown felt hat, crown with flat top, turned-up brim. 3 Navy-blue straw hat, shallow crown, wide brim. 4 Brown leather sling-back strap sandals, low heels, open toes. 5 Cherry-red felt hat, moulded crown, turned-up brim. 6 Navy-blue and white leather shoes, half-and-half design, almond-shaped toes. 7 White knitted-wool beret, red and black pattern, matching scarf. 8 Green leather step-in shoes, knotted thong detail, low heels. 9 Half-and-half red and navy-blue peep-toe shoes. 10 Beige suede shoes, open sides, narrow strap fastening, peep toes, low semi-wedge heels. 11 Orange-red leather lace-up shoes, flat heels. 12 Brown leather shoes, cream mesh fronts, peep toes, high tapered heels. 13 Brown felt hat, fur trim. 14 Grey leather clutch bag, shaped flap threaded through self-leather strap, top-stitched trim. 15 Dark-red leather handbag, flap, short handle, top-stitched detail. 16 Black leather shoes, high tapered heels, almond-shaped toes. 17 Wine-red shoulder bag, scalloped flap embroidered in gold thread. 18 Lime-green wool beret. 19 Cream leather ankle boots, wide turned-down cuffs. 20 Black leather sling-back shoes, bow trim, high tapered heels. 21 Blue velvet slippers, red quilted silk linings, gold monogram. 22 Brown leather step-in shoes, rounded tongues, self-leather strap trim, top-stitched detail. 23 Black leather boots, self-leather stirrup trim, side-zip fastening. 24 Brown leather step-in shoes, square tongues, inset bands of green and grey over instep. 25 White leather knee-high boots, top-stitched in gold thread on cuffs and above ankle seam, almond-shaped toes, high tapered heels. 26 White leather bag, flap, gold thread embroidery, long adjustable handle.

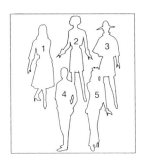
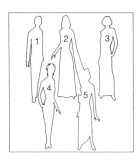
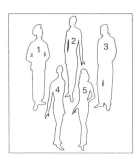
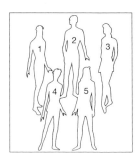

1982 Day Wear

1 Single-breasted beige suede jacket, self-suede button fastening from hemline to under stand collar, deep yoke, padded shoulders, drop head three-quarter-length inset sleeves gathered into narrow cuffs, top-stitched edges and detail, dark-blue leather belt, stepped buckle fastening. Knee-length bright-pink wool gathered skirt. Dark-blue leather strap sandals, high spike heels. **2** Charcoal-grey linen dress, bloused bodice, concealed strap fastening, plain white collar, matching cuffs of full-length inset sleeves, box-pleat detail from padded shoulders to wrists, above-knee-level straight skirt, buckled black leather belt. Black leather strap sandals. **3** Black and white striped knitted-wool three-piece suit: above knee-length edge-to-edge collarless coat, three-quarter-length kimono-style sleeves with seams, edges and hems bound in black; long sweater top, low V-shaped neckline; plain-black above-knee-length straight skirt. Black lacquered-straw hat, high crown, wide straight brim. Black leather shoes, almond-shaped toes, high straight heels. **4** Pale-blue, grey and white striped cotton jacket, single-breasted two-button fastening, narrow lapels, full-length sleeves worn pushed up to elbow-level, piped pockets. Tapered pale-blue cotton trousers, no turn-ups, dark-blue leather belt. Pale-grey cotton collar-attached shirt, concealed strap fastening, single breast patch pocket; red, grey and blue spotted silk bow-tie. Dark-blue leather step-in shoes. **5** Dark-red wool two-piece suit: double-breasted hip-length jacket, notched shawl collar, padded shoulders, full-length inset sleeves, piped pockets; straight-cut trousers, no creases or turn-ups. White silk collarless T-shirt. Black leather strap sandals, high straight heels.

Evening Wear

1 Dark-blue wool and mohair two-piece evening suit: long double-breasted jacket, wide lapels faced in blue silk, matching covered buttons and piped pockets; tapered trousers, no turn-ups. White silk collar-attached shirt, dark-blue velvet bow-tie. Dark-blue leather step-in shoes. **2** Ground-length white silk-chiffon evening dress, layered skirt gathered from base of hip-length white guipure-lace fitted and boned strapless bodice, ground-length white silk-chiffon stole worn across throat to trail at back. White satin shoes. **3** Fine silk-satin evening dress patterned in various purples, oranges and reds, fitted strapless boned bodice horizontally ruched to hip-level at one side. Purple satin strap sandals, ruched fronts, peep toes, ankle straps, high heels. **4** Strapless red silk-jersey cocktail dress, hip-length fitted strapless bodice, gold bead embroidery following lines of low neckline, above-knee-length wrapover draped skirt. Gold kid strap sandals, ankle straps, high heels. **5** Silk-taffeta evening dress, lower part of fitted and boned strapless bodice in dark blue, upper bodice with centre-front split in pale lilac-grey, matching ankle-length skirt, wide sweeping curved slash to knee-level at one side, narrow fuchsia-pink belt trimmed on centre front with outsized bow. Lilac-grey satin shoes, peep toes.

Sports and Leisure Wear

1 Jogging. Pink cotton-jersey two-piece suit: hip-length bloused jacket, large half-circle patch pockets, front-zip fastening from hem to under ribbed charcoal-grey stand collar, matching elasticated ribbing on hem, cuffs of full-length raglan sleeves and cuffs of ankle-length unfitted trousers. White canvas lace-up trainers. **2** Swimwear. Dark-plum-red Lycra swimsuit, low V-shaped neckline formed between wide halter straps, ruched detail at base of side seams above high-cut legs. **3** Casual wear. Pale-yellow knitted-cotton sweater, high round neckline, blue and white striped trim, matching heads of full-length inset sleeves, ribbed cuffs matching hemline. Tapered cream cotton trousers, pleated from waistband, side-hip pockets, wide turn-ups. Cream cotton collar-attached shirt, collar worn open. Dark-cream leather lace-up shoes. **4** Surfing. Black Lycra all-in-one suit, low-cut armholes, wide shoulder straps, Velcro fastenings, V-shaped insert of purple and yellow stripes under low scooped neckline, matching stripes on lower front leg patches, all edges and detail outlined in lilac. **5** Beach wear. White Lycra poolside swimsuit, draped halter straps, deep V-shaped neckline, wrapover above waistline, low back, high-cut legs, self-fabric belt, gold clasp fastening.

Underwear

1 White elasticated-cotton strapless bra, underwired and padded cups, white cotton-lace trim, back fastening. White Lycra pantie-girdle, deep waistband, top-stitched front-firming panel, long legs, fine tuck trim. **2** White knitted-cotton briefs, elasticated waistband, double fabric front panel, Y-shaped stitched seams, high-cut legs. **3** Primrose-yellow silk chemise top, self-fabric rouleau shoulder straps, low scalloped neckline edged with wide panel of embroidered and lace-trimmed white silk-satin, matching hems of wide flared knickers, cut high on side seams, gathers from elasticated waistline. **4** Peach-pink Lycra bra, underwired cups cut in one with adjustable shoulder straps, side padding, wide lace trim, back fastening. Peach-pink silk knickers, flared legs, high cut on side seams, scalloped lace trim, gathers from elasticated waistline. **5** Black silk-satin mini-length slip, panel seams from under fitted cups, inset black embroidered lace under bust, matching trim above low neckline and on flared hemline, adjustable shoulder straps.

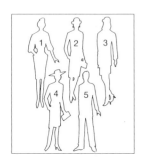

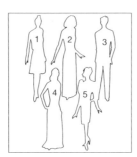

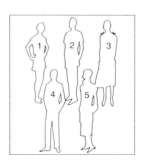

1983 Day Wear

1 Green silk blouse patterned with self-colour satin leaves, blouse bodice draped from button fastening on padded shoulders, three-quarter-length inset sleeves gathered on shoulders and into cuffs. Above-knee-length dark-green wool skirt, pockets set into hip-level pleats, black suede belt. Black leather shoes, almond-shaped toes. **2** Brown, grey and black striped wool coat-dress, double-breasted fastening, pointed lapels and collar, side panel seams, breast pockets, hip-level pockets set into side seams, padded shoulders, full-length inset sleeves. Grey felt hat, high crown, self-colour petersham band, curled brim. **3** Three-quarter-length camel-coloured wool coat, double-breasted fastening, wide lapels, long collar, hip-level welt pockets, full-length two-piece sleeves, padded shoulders, top-stitched edges and detail. Emerald-green wool polo-neck sweater-dress, straight above-knee-length skirt. Navy-blue leather gloves and knee-high fitted boots, pointed toes, high heels, side-zip fastening. **4** Cherry-red wool two-piece suit: short fitted jacket, double-breasted fastening, wide lapels, padded shoulders, full-length inset sleeves, button trim above hem; straight above-knee-length skirt, pleats from waist. Black silk blouse, high round neckline. Black straw hat, shallow crown, self-colour petersham band, wide brim. Large black leather clutch bag. Cherry-red leather sling-back shoes, almond-shaped toes, high heels. **5** Cream linen-tweed two-piece suit: long double-breasted jacket, inset half-belt from side seam to side seam, large patch pockets, wide shoulder, top-stitched edges and detail; tapered trousers, turn-ups. Pale-cream linen collar-attached shirt. Pink silk tie and pocket handkerchief. Light-brown leather lace-up brogues.

Evening Wear

1 Royal-blue acetate-jersey cocktail dress, bloused bodice, fine self-fabric rouleau shoulder straps, low scalloped neckline edged in tiny gold beads to match centre-front seam, above-knee-length accordion-pleated skirt, mock ties from side waist. Gold kid strap sandals. **2** Fuchsia-pink silk-chiffon evening dress, pleated halter cross-over straps form upper part of fitted and draped bodice, matching shaped hip sash and front fall, multilayered ground-length full skirt. **3** Cream silk evening jacket, single-breasted one-button fastening, double-breasted lapels faced with cream satin, piped pockets. Tapered black wool trousers, no turn-ups. White silk shirt, attached wing collar. Black silk-satin bow-tie. Black kid lace-up shoes. **4** Gold lamé evening dress, fitted bias-cut bodice, drapery from central knot over wired cups, draped shoulder straps and hip sash with waterfall ends, ground-length bias-cut skirt. **5** Cocktail dress, royal-blue silk-velvet bodice and above-knee-length straight skirt cut without waist seam, upper bodice draped in black silk-taffeta, wide off-the-shoulder low V-shaped neckline, point trimmed with large black taffeta bow, outsized puff sleeves gathered into deep cuffs. Black silk shoes, pointed toes, high straight heels.

Sports and Leisure Wear

1 Tennis. Waist-length white cotton blouse, low square neckline, cap sleeves, top-stitched edges. White cotton-poplin tailored shorts, flared legs, turn-ups. White knitted-cotton socks, white canvas lace-up sports shoes. **2** Tennis. White knitted-cotton shirt; collar, strap fastening and short inset sleeves in dark-blue knitted cotton. White cotton-poplin tailored shorts, buttoned waistband, side-hip pockets, red and blue logo on outside leg above hemline at one side. White knitted-cotton socks, white trainers. **3** Holiday wear. Yellow and white striped cotton sundress, straight hip-length bodice with horizontal stripes, straight neckline bound with vertically striped band, matching below-knee-length gathered skirt, large horizontally-striped patch pockets, narrow self-fabric shoulder straps, bow-ties on shoulders. Yellow canvas pumps, decorative laces. **4** Golf. Beige and cream knitted-wool collarless cardigan, single-breasted fastening, ribbed edges matching cuffs of full-length inset sleeves and edges of three patch pockets. Light-brown wool tapered trousers, side-hip pockets, turn-ups. Cream, brown and green checked brushed-cotton shirt. Brown leather step-in shoes. **5** Country wear. Olive-green knitted-wool two-piece jumper suit: long top, deep ribbed hem, cable-stitched front panel, matching detail above ribbed hems of full-length inset sleeves, cable repeated on dropped shoulderline, padded shoulders; straight mid-calf-length skirt. Nut-brown wool scarf, fringed ends, matching pull-on knitted-wool hat with ribbed edge. Matching wool tights. Dark-brown-green leather lace-up shoes, almond-shaped toes, flat heels.

Accessories

1 White leather shoes, blue striped trim on toes and low wedge heels. **2** Red felt hat, wide brim. **3** Cream leather shoes, brown trim, almond-shaped toes, tapered heels. **4** Brown mock-snakeskin boots, ruched above ankles, low tapered heels. **5** Grey leather shoes, low wedge heels. **6** Asymmetric sling-back red leather sandals, wide front strap, black braid trim, peep toes, high spike heels. **7** Black leather shoes, high straight heels. **8** Beige leather sandals, single front strap, ankle strap, buckle fastening, tapered heels. **9** Yellow leather shoes, asymmetric open sides, ruched fronts, open toes, low wedge heels. **10** Black knitted-wool pull-on hat, stalk trim. **11** Tan leather boots, ruched on ankles above decorative seaming, mock-snakeskin inset collar, low heels. **12** Green strap sandals, low wedge heels. **13** Navy-blue leather shoes, fronts trimmed white, matching sling-back bag, flap, stud fastening, long strap. **14** Gold-brown bag, flap, stud fastening, long strap. **15** Black leather strap sandals, high tapered heels. **16** Maroon-red canvas bag, double flap, stud fastening, long handle. **17** Yellow straw hat, low crown, flat top, blue ribbon band, wide flat brim. **18** Knee-high black leather boots, ruched on ankles, low tapered heels. **19** Off-white plastic leather-look clutch bag, suede-look trim. **20** Unstructured white felt hat, high crown, black band, wide brim. **21** Brown leather step-in shoes, grey and tan inset trim. **22** Black leather step-in shoes, mock tie, fringed ends. **23** Dark-grey leather step-in shoes, self-leather crossed strap detail. **24** Black leather step-in shoes, high tongues, bar straps, cut-out detail. **25** Black leather shoes, laced through metal rings, decorative seaming. **26** Green leather moccasins, self-leather laces. **27** Ankle-high white trainers, Velcro fastenings.

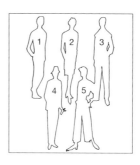
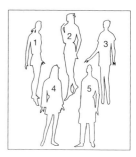

1984 Day Wear

1 Grey, brown and black checked wool- and silk-tweed jacket, double-breasted fastening, wide lapels, padded shoulders, full-length inset sleeves, hip-level piped pockets. Above-knee-length straight skirt, centre-front unpressed knife-pleat. Black leather shoes, pointed toes, high heels. 2 Short black leather jacket, zip fastening to under collar with decorative ring-and-strap fastening, matching epaulettes, sleeves gathered into cuffs, V-shaped tucked seam from centre-shoulder to centre-front of hip band, diagonal piped pockets. Fitted blue denim jeans, top-stitched edges and detail. White cotton T-shirt. Black leather cowboy boots, pointed toes, stacked heels. 3 Collarless yellow crepe dress, blue and grey random pattern, box-pleated bloused bodice, centre-front button fastening to under high round neckline, padded shoulders, inset sleeves gathered into deep cuffs, knee-length skirt, unpressed pleats over hips, centre-front box-pleat, self-fabric belt gathered through ring. Grey leather bag, matching shoes, pointed toes, high stiletto heels. 4 Beige wool three-piece suit: long unfitted edge-to-edge jacket, wide lapels, full-length kimono-style sleeves, wide turned-back cuffs, padded shoulders, top-stitched edges and detail; collarless waistcoat, pointed edges knotted to form fastening; mid-calf-length skirt, hip-level pockets in side seams. Cream knitted-silk-tweed collarless sweater. Cream wool beret. Brown and beige leather lace-up shoes. 5 Cream wool dress flecked with navy-blue, bloused bodice and full-length cuffed sleeves cut in one piece, draped cowl neckline, padded shoulders, gathered skirt, side-hip pockets, navy-blue woven plastic belt, large round buckle. Blue and white patterned turban. Navy-blue plastic strap sandals.

Wedding Wear

1 Pink silk-moiré taffeta three-piece wedding suit: collarless fitted jacket, single-breasted fastening from waist seam to under bustline, wide neckline split to show low neckline of blouse, padded shoulders, three-quarter-length inset sleeves gathered into narrow cuffs, short peplum; ground-length flared skirt, centre-front mock-button fastening. Pillbox hat matching suit fabric, short silk-tulle veil. 2 Ivory-white silk-jersey wedding dress, four tiers of wrapover curved panels, top-stitched edges, fitted bodice, slashed neckline, padded shoulders, full-length inset sleeves fitted from wrist to elbow, ground-length flared skirt. Layered ivory-white silk-organdie crownless hat trimmed with silk flowers. 3 White silk-satin wedding dress, fitted bodice draped from centre-front padded motif to follow lines of wide V-shaped off-the-shoulder neckline, padded motif and drapery repeated on the puffed sleeves, bead edging matching neckline and pointed waist seam, lace undersleeves, ground-length gathered skirt worn over stiffened petticoats. Beaded white satin headdress, long silk-tulle veil. Long white stretch-satin gloves. 4 Pale-cream fine wool wedding dress, unfitted hip-length bodice, diagonal tucked decoration, high round neckline, padded shoulders, full-length inset sleeves, gathered on head, buttons from wrist to below elbow-level, ground-length skirt gathered from hip seam. Silk flower headdress, long silk-tulle veil. 5 Three-piece morning suit: single-breasted dark-grey wool tailcoat, single-button fastening, double-breasted lapels; light-grey wool collarless waistcoat; charcoal-grey and black striped wool tapered trousers, no turn-ups. White cotton shirt worn with wing collar and silver-grey and black patterned silk cravat. Black leather lace-up shoes.

Sports and Leisure Wear

1 Exercise wear. Sleeveless blue and white striped cotton vest, low scooped neckline. Navy-blue cotton-jersey trousers, tapered legs, pockets set into top-stitched side seams, pleats from buttoned waistband, pintucked central creases. White trainers. 2 Country wear. Burnt-orange wool three-piece suit: long collarless coat-jacket, single-breasted fastening with suede-covered buttons, padded shoulders, full-length inset sleeves, large hip-level patch pockets; sweater with low V-shaped neckline; straight above-knee-length skirt, top-stitched edges and detail. Orange stretch-wool turban. Long tan leather boots, ruched at ankle, almond-shaped toes, low tapered heels. 3 Casual wear. Grey knitted-wool sweater, low V-shaped neckline, deep ribbed edge, matching hemline and short cap sleeves. Blue-grey wool tapered trousers, side-hip pockets, no turn-ups. Green, turquoise and grey checked wool collar-attached shirt. Black leather step-in shoes. 4 Golf. Brown and brick-red checked wool single-breasted jacket, wide lapels, brown suede collar, matching yoke and covered button, large patch pockets, padded shoulders, full-length inset sleeves. Cream wool shirt, flat wrapover collar above mock boiled-front. Dark-cream wool trousers, wide waistband, brown suede belt, buttoned loops, tapered legs, wide turn-ups. Brown suede gloves, matching step-in shoes, fringe trim. 5 Holiday wear. Waist-length yellow cotton jacket, asymmetric fastening, double-breasted on hemline, single-breasted on stand collar, padded shoulders, three-quarter-length inset cuffed sleeves, box-pleat decoration. Ankle-length black cotton trousers, deep waistband, button fastening, wide legs, off-centre knife-pleats. Black leather strap sandals, low heels.

Underwear and Negligee

1 Lilac polyester-satin strapless camiknickers, elasticated neckline edged with wide scalloped lace to match front panel and hems of straight-cut legs, elasticated drawstring waist, crotch fastening. 2 Royal-blue polyester-satin camiknickers, low V-shaped neckline formed by cross-over bloused bodice, elasticated waist seam, asymmetric overskirt with curved edge, high-cut legs, self-fabric rouleau shoulder straps, all main edges trimmed with self-colour polyester lace. 3 Hip-length pale-pink silk nightshirt, short sleeves cut in one with body, narrow pale-blue stitched cuffs, matching collar and short pointed wrapover front panel, hemline curves up to side seams, top-stitched edges and detail. 4 Pale-blue shiny acetate and nylon kimono-inspired dressing gown, patterned with random dull self-colour stripes and bright-blue flowers, wrapover front, wide self-fabric bindings, matching tie-belt, padded shoulders, full-length kimono-style sleeves gathered into narrow cuffs, mini-length skirts. 5 Red polyester-satin dressing gown, wrapover front, wide shawl collar, full-length inset sleeves worn pushed up to elbow-level, self-fabric tie-belt, large hip-level patch pockets, top-stitched edges and detail. Black polyester-satin pyjama trousers.

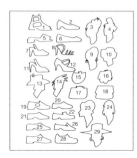

1985 Day Wear

1 Black showerproofed cotton topcoat, single-breasted fastening, inset sleeves, strap-and-button trim, matching epaulettes, saddle-stitched trim. Double-breasted dark-salmon-pink cotton jacket, narrow lapels, piped pockets. Grey and blue checked cotton tapered trousers, no turn-ups. Grey cotton collar-attached shirt, gold and blue striped polyester tie. Navy-blue step-in shoes. **2** Grey knitted-wool two-piece jumper suit: long unfitted top, wide neckline, padded shoulders, deep inset sleeves, button trim on top-stitched side seams above hemline, matching detail on shoulders, above-knee-length straight skirt. Black leather shoes. **3** Edge-to-edge mustard-yellow and black flecked wool-tweed jacket, padded shoulders, wide cap sleeves, high stand collar, triangular-shaped patch pockets, top-stitched edges and detail. Hip-length collarless black wool shirt, full-length cuffed sleeves. Mid-calf-length mustard-yellow wool straight skirt, inset front panel. Black ribbed-wool tights, black leather pumps, flat heels. **4** Camel-coloured wool coat, wrapover front, self-fabric tie-belt, wide lapels, large collar, padded shoulders, full-length raglan sleeves, split cuffs, large patch pockets, top-stitched edges and detail. Black and terracotta checked wool single-breasted jacket, wide lapels, flap pockets. Black wool polo-neck sweater. Black wool straight mini-skirt. Black leather shoes, almond-shaped toes, medium-high tapered heels. **5** Grey and white striped polyester and cotton dress, bloused bodice, yoke, decorative front panel, padded shoulders, short inset sleeves, stitched cuffs, low V-shaped neckline, plain white collar, black satin bow trim, mid-calf-length panelled skirt, box-pleat hem, side-hip pockets. Grey leather lace-up shoes.

Evening Wear

1 Black wool and silk three-piece evening suit: single-breasted jacket, single-button fastening, double-breasted lapels faced with black silk, piped pockets; collarless single-breasted waistcoat, straight hemline; tapered tousers, black silk braid trim on outside seam, no turn-ups. White silk shirt, attached wing collar; black silk bow-tie. Black patent-leather lace-up shoes. **2** Royal-blue silk-jersey evening dress, draped bodice and ground-length skirt cut without waist seam, wide and low sweetheart neckline, padded shoulders, full-length bishop-style sleeves gathered into deep cuffs. **3** Bright-green silk-chiffon cocktail dress, draped and ruched from low neckline of boned strapless bodice to hemline of mini-length skirt. Long black stretch-satin gloves. Black satin sling-back strap sandals, high stiletto heels. **4** Ink-blue silk-jersey evening dress, bias-cut wrapover bodice and skirt draped from self-fabric knot at base of low asymmetric neckline, hemline below-knee-length at front and ankle-length at back, short inset sleeves, padded shoulders. Gold kid strap sandals, asymmetric sling-back straps, high spike heels. **5** Fuchsia-pink silk evening dress, low neckline, fitted strapless boned bodice, draped and ruched from central seam to low hip-level, ground-length skirt flared from hip-level, godet of unpressed pleats centre-front hip-level.

Sports and Leisure Wear

1 Tennis. Hip-length white knitted-cotton unfitted T-shaped top, short wide sleeves, narrow turned-back cuffs, flat peter-pan collar, offset strap with concealed fastening, hip-level band. Knee-length white cotton skirt, unpressed knife-pleats from waist. White stretch-cotton towelling headband. White canvas step-in shoes, elasticated sides, rubber soles, round toes, short white cotton socks.
2 Holiday wear. Pale-grey knitted-cotton T-shaped sweater-dress, wide round neckline, top-stitched facings above manufacturer's logo, padded shoulders, full-length sleeves cut in one with unfitted bodice, top-stitched hems, large hip-level patch pockets, top-stitched cuffs, straight knee-length skirt, no waist seam. White cotton peaked cap. White leather step-in strap sandals, round toes, flat heels. **3** Beach wear. Hip-length pink knitted-cotton sleeveless vest, top-stitched low neckline, matching deep armholes, printed logo across chest, top-stitched hem. Pink knitted-cotton shorts, wide legs, top-stitched hems. **4** Tennis. Collarless white knitted-cotton shirt, high round neckline, top-stitched edge, short cloth-bound fly fastening, two-button fastening, full-length inset sleeves worn pushed up to elbow-level, dropped shoulder seam. White cotton shorts, short legs, curved wrapover side seams, inset pockets, fly front, top-stitched edges and detail. White knitted-cotton ankle socks, white canvas tennis shoes, rubber soles. **5** Beach wear. Waist-length yellow knitted-cotton vest, wide neckline, top-stitched edges, matching deep armholes and hemline. Blue cotton-poplin shorts, pleats from waist, side-hip pockets, short legs, top-stitched.

Accessories

1 Yellow leather strap sandals, double strap-and-buckle fastening, open sides, flat heels. **2** Brown suede shoes, low heels. **3** Red cotton-towelling turban. **4** White Lycra turban, large bow trim. **5** Tan leather mules, open toes, low stacked heels. **6** Red leather shoes, low wedge heels. **7** Navy-blue sling-back shoes, tapered heels. **8** Green leather strap sandals, asymmetric sling-back straps, stiletto heels. **9** Red wool beret. **10** Cream felt hat, high crown, turned-back brim.**11** Grey leather sling-back shoes, black patent-leather toecaps and heels. **12** Beige suede shoes, asymmetric cross straps, tapered heels. **13** White felt hat, high crown, draped black taffeta band and bow, wide brim. **14** Brimless grey felt hat, black feather trim. **15** Black silk evening bag, gold clasp fastening and trim. **16** Cream satin shell-shaped evening bag, embroidered pearl beads, clasp fastening. **17** Black suede clutch bag, flap with central ruched detail. **18** Brown leather clutch bag, green and black inset trim. **19** Brown leather sandals, open sides, strap-and-buckle fastening, perforated fronts. **20** Navy-blue canvas step-in beach shoes, rope soles. **21** Grey leather step-in shoes, top-stitched detail, button trim. **22** Black leather step-in shoes, top-stitched detail, button trim. **23** Pale-grey felt hat, large crown, wide black band, narrow turned-up brim. **24** Red wool fitted hat, turned-back brim. **25** Brown leather lace-up shoes, top-stitched edges. **26** White leather sandals, strap fronts, strap-and-buckle fastening. **27** White trainers, blue side flashes. **28** White trainers, red striped flashes. **29** Black felt hat, high flat crown, wide brim.

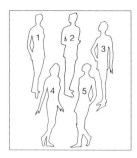

1986 Day Wear

1 Oatmeal and beige silk-tweed collarless jacket, asymmetric two-button fastening on hip-level below wide self-binding of front edges and neckline, padded shoulders, full-length inset sleeves, button trim on wrists, hip-level welt pockets. Narrow dark-beige wool-and-silk mixture trousers. Cream silk collarless blouse, wrapover neckline, self-fabric binding, button trim. Beige leather strap sandals. 2 Below-knee-length camel-coloured wool coat, double-breasted fastening from hip-level to under wide-set collar, padded shoulders, full-length raglan sleeves, rounded split seams at wrist-level, hip-level bound pockets, top-stitched edges and detail. Black leather beret, matching shoes, almond-shaped toes, tapered heels. Beige leather gloves. 3 Charcoal-grey wool two-piece suit: hip-length fitted single-breasted jacket, two-button fastening, rounded wide lapels, matching collar and cuffs of full-length inset sleeves, padded shoulders, below-waist-level welt pockets; above-knee-level straight skirt, hem rounded up to centre-front. Black leather sling-back shoes, almond-shaped toes, medium-high tapered heels. 4 Short fitted collarless wool jacket, all-over pattern of blues, greys and pinks, asymmetric fastening from waist-level to above bustline, padded shoulders, full-length sleeves gathered into armholes, top-stitched edges and detail. Accordion-pleated blue and grey wool mid-calf-length skirt. Wine-red leather boots, almond-shaped toes. 5 Knee-length camel-coloured wool overcoat, single-breasted one-button fastening, wide lapels, padded shoulders, hip-level welt pockets. Black wool tapered trousers, no turn-ups. Dark-beige wool collar-attached shirt. Grey and blue striped silk tie. Black leather gloves; matching shoes, strap-and-buckle trim.

Evening Wear

1 Silver-grey silk-chiffon strapless blouse, blue and pink flocked-velvet flower pattern, boned bodice wrapover drapery to large self-fabric bow on side-hip. Navy-blue ankle-length straight skirt. Side split from hemline to knee-level at one side. Navy-blue silk shoes, almond-shaped toes, low tapered heels. 2 Black silk two-piece suit: double-breasted jacket, wide lapels faced in satin, matching covered buttons, piped pockets, tapered trousers, no turn-ups. Red silk collar-attached shirt worn without tie, matching red silk handkerchief in breast pocket. Black suede lace-up shoes. 3 Yellow polyester-chiffon cocktail dress, spotted in red, fitted and draped hip-length strapless bodice, red velvet ribbon belt, bow-tie on one side, gathered three-tier skirt to above knee-length, worn over stiffened petticoats. Red satin shoes, pointed toes, stiletto heels. 4 Bright-pink, crinkle-pleated silk-satin evening dress, fitted bodice, padded shoulders, short cap sleeves, black satin polo collar, matching wide belt, flared ankle-length skirt. Above-elbow-length black stretch-satin gloves. Black satin shoes, pointed toes, high stiletto heels. 5 Smoke-blue and charcoal-grey striped silk blouse, fitted bodice, off-the-shoulder neckline, cuffed edge. Above-knee-length cerise-pink silk-taffeta gathered skirt, worn over navy-blue silk petticoats with scalloped hems, wide buckled belt in matching fabric. Navy-blue satin shoes, pointed toes, high stiletto heels.

Sports and Leisure Wear

1 Casual wear. Pale-turquoise unstructured cotton jacket, two-button single-breasted fastening, wide lapels, patch pockets. Cream cotton tapered trousers, side-hip pockets, no creases or turn-ups. Turquoise knitted-cotton collar-attached shirt. Light-brown leather shoes, strap-and-buckle fastening. 2 Exercise wear. Pale-grey knitted-cotton T-shirt. Grey knitted-cotton jogging pants, gathered from elasticated waistband, mock fly opening, side-hip pockets, tapered legs gathered into elasticated band at ankle-level. White trainers, Velcro strap fastenings. 3 Country wear. Brown wool-tweed single-breasted jacket, wide lapels, brown velvet collar, patch pockets. Mid-calf-length light-brown wool skirt, unpressed pleats from waist, centre-front inverted box-pleat, brown leather belt. Collarless knitted-wool waistcoat, brown, black and mustard pattern, single-breasted fastening, plain brown ribbed edging. Cream and brown checked brushed-cotton shirt, attached collar worn open; brown and black patterned silk scarf. Dark-brown leather boots, front lacing, almond-shaped toes, flat heels. 4 Beach wear. Blue and white printed cotton two-piece beach suit: strapless bra top, fabric draped over wired cups and through centre-front knot of fabric; knee-length wrapover skirt, loop-and-button fastening at one side of curved waistband, asymmetric drapery from waistband to side hip. 5 Exercise wear. Royal-blue cotton-velour two-piece leisure suit: hip-length unfitted jacket, zip fastening from hipband to under pointed collar, padded shoulders, inset sleeves gathered into stretch cuffs, patch pockets set into top-stitched panel seams; unfitted pants gathered from waist and into stretch cuffs on ankles. White canvas pumps, elasticated front panels, rubber soles.

Underwear

1 White Lycra bra, underwired, formed and seamed cups, light underpadding, lace trim, adjustable shoulder straps, back fastening. White cotton and Lycra briefs, high-cut legs, cross-over side panels, double fabric front V-shaped panel, lace trim. 2 White cotton-polyester boxer shorts, patterned with outsized red, blue and yellow spots, elasticated waistband, open fly fronts, wide legs, side seams split above hemline. 3 Fine cream cotton and Lycra-lace mini-slip, low scalloped neckline, matching hemline, cream satin rouleau shoulder straps and underarm bindings, flesh-coloured briefs, high-cut legs on sides to elasticated waistband. 4 Black Lycra and Lycra-lace body suit, bra top draped with plain black Lycra from centre-front under bust to above waist-level on sides to low back, low neckline, narrow Lycra shoulder straps, bow trim, main body in stretch-Lycra-lace, high-cut legs trimmed with fine lace edging, matching under arm to back, fastening under crotch. 5 White stretch-Lycra-lace bodysuit, deep plunge neckline to waist-level, scalloped edges, infilled with plain white Lycra, matching adjustable shoulder straps and underarm binding, high-cut legs, fastening under crotch.

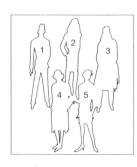

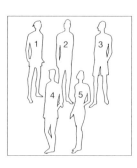

1987 Day Wear

1 Charcoal-grey and blue striped wool two-piece suit: single-breasted fitted jacket, single-button fastening, wide lapels, padded shoulders, full-length inset sleeves, flap pockets; tapered trousers, pleats from waistband, blue leather belt. Knitted charcoal-grey wool polo-neck sweater. Brimless charcoal-grey wool hat. Black leather boots. 2 Dark-grey two-piece suit: waist-length single-breasted jacket, two-button fastening, wide stitched band around hem, brooch trim on centre-front, narrow lapels, padded shoulders, full-length inset sleeves gathered into cuffs; high waistband and mini-skirt cut in one piece, vertical panel seams. Black leather shoes, medium-high tapered heels. 3 Below-knee-length sage-green wool overcoat, wrapover front, self-fabric tie-belt, wide lapels with buttonholes, large collar, raglan sleeves, buttoned flaps at wrist-level, flap pockets, top-stitched edges and detail. Green and brown flecked wool-tweed single-breasted jacket, patch pockets. Dark-green-brown wool tapered trousers, pleats from waist, side-hip pockets, no turn-ups. Cream cotton collar-attached shirt, buttoned-down pointed collar. Brown wool tie. Brown leather lace-up shoes. 4 Red knitted-wool three-piece suit: below-knee-length edge-to-edge coat, roll collar, padded shoulders, sleeves gathered at wrists, large hip-level patch pockets; hip-length polo-neck sweater, self-fabric buckled belt; straight mini-length skirt. Dark-grey wool tights. Deep-red suede lace-up shoes, ridged thick soles, flat heels. 5 Scarlet wool-jersey mini-dress, high round neckline, facings top-stitched to match cuffs of three-quarter-length sleeves and inset seam, padded shoulders, black patent-leather hip-level belt. Black patent-leather sling-back shoes.

Wedding Wear

1 White silk-jersey wedding dress, fitted bodice and ground-length flared skirt cut without waist seam, upper bodice draped with self-fabric cross-over panel, white silk-organdie off-the-shoulder collar. Hair decorated with fresh flowers. Full-length stretch-silk gloves. 2 Pale-cream silk-jersey wedding dress, strapless bloused bodice, ground-length flared skirt, transparent cream silk bloused overbodice patterned with cream flocked-velvet flower pattern, slashed neckline, cap sleeves, self-fabric sash draped over hips, gathered front panel to hemline of dress. Cream silk bow hair decoration. Three-quarter-length stretch-fabric gloves. 3 White silk three-piece wedding suit: short edge-to-edge jacket, curved front edges, grown-on collar, padded shoulder, full-length leg-of-mutton-style sleeves; chemise blouse, straight neckline; ankle-length flared skirt, wide waistband, large bow trim on centre-front. 4 White silk wedding dress, fitted bodice, low scooped neckline, full-length leg-of-mutton sleeves, lace trim above and below bow-trimmed waist-belt, matching edging on long detachable train, ground-length straight skirt. Long silk-tulle veil scattered with silk flowers. 5 Ivory-white silk wedding dress, hip-length fitted bodice, self-fabric covered buttons on centre-front from under bow trim on bustline to pointed hip seam, off-the-shoulder neckline and cap sleeves with scalloped edges which match hemline of full-length gathered skirt. Full-length stretch-fabric gloves.

Sports and Leisure Wear

1 Tennis. Mini-length white polyester-cotton dress, semi-fitted bodice and flared skirt cut without waist seam, high round neckline, collar split at front to red braid trim above bustline, matching braid trim on hip-level asymmetric patch pockets and armhole bindings. White cotton socks, white canvas tennis shoes. 2 Jogging. Light-blue knitted-cotton vest, high round neckline, cut-away armholes and hemline with top-stitched edges and seams. Black canvas running shoes. 3 Beach wear. Yellow polyester and cotton shorts, orange stripes set into side panels, matching inside legs and buttoned waistband. 4 Tennis. White knitted-cotton shirt, pointed collar, strap fastening, short inset sleeves, stitched cuffs, multicolour printed geometric pattern across chest. White cotton tailored shorts, waistband with adjustable buttoned side straps, short legs split on side seams above hemline, side-hip pockets lined in blue. White cotton socks patterned with fine blue stripes and manufacturer's logo, white canvas tennis shoes. 5 Beach wear. Gold Lycra one-piece swimsuit, bra top moulded and seamed, underwired cups cut in one with wide shoulder straps, high-cut legs, top-stitched edges and seams.

Accessories

1 Yellow ostrich leather bag, front flap, strap-and-clasp fastening, short handle. 2 Beige leather sling-back shoes, high vamps, cut-away front, high tapered heels. 3 Natural straw hat, blue band. 4 Red leather bucket-shaped bag, strap-and-stud fastening, long handle, top-stitched trim. 5 Tan leather step-in shoes, tassel trim, round toes, flat heels. 6 Cream leather shoulder bag, green and brown trim, long handle. 7 Brown leather shoes, high tapered heels. 8 Grey leather shoulder bag, blue and red trim, long handle. 9 Wine-red felt hat, self-felt leaves in brim. 10 Black felt hat, high crown, draped white silk band, wide brim. 11 Black leather sling-back shoes, medium-high tapered heels. 12 Black leather shoes, red suede shaped inset, stiletto heels. 13 Beige suede sling-back shoes, high vamps, flat heels. 14 Red leather shoes, silver inset stripe above heels, matching toecaps and tapered heels. 15 Black quilted-leather shoulder bag, chain handle. 16 Brown crocodile clutch bag. 17 White straw hat, shallow crown, black band, wide brim. 18 Cream straw hat, shallow crown, red band, matching edges of wide brim and bow trim. 19 Dark-grey leather clutch bag, flap, two strap-and-stud fastenings. 20 Black suede shoes, scalloped edges, tapered heels. 21 White straw hat, high crown, flat top, petersham band and bow, wide brim. 22 Brown leather step-in shoes, strap-and-button trim, elasticated sides, flat heels. 23 Red velvet hair decoration, petersham bow trim. 24 Red suede ankle boots, trimmed self-suede bows, louis heels. 25 Black leather lace-up ankle boots, fake-fur trim, louis heels. 26 Black leather elastic-sided ankle boots, medium-high tapered heels. 27 Tan leather pumps, flat heels. 28 Black leather shoes, petersham bow trim.

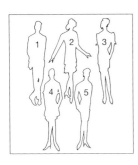

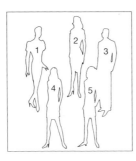

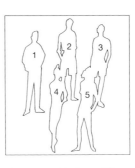

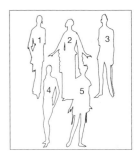

1988 Day Wear

1 Black and blue-grey checked wool-tweed jacket, single-breasted fastening, narrow lapels, flap pockets. Yellow knitted-wool collarless cardigan, single-breasted button fastening, welt pockets. Blue denim tapered jeans, side-hip pockets, top-stitched edges and seams. Pale-blue cotton collar-attached shirt. Red and blue patterned silk tie. Black leather lace-up ankle boots. **2** Brown and beige checked-pattern linen jacket, single-breasted concealed fastening, hip-level button trim, high round neckline, padded shoulders, full-length inset sleeves, button trim on wrists, hip-level piped pockets. Two-tier mini-length pleated linen skirt, brown and beige leaf pattern. Brown leather shoes, almond-shaped toes, tapered heels. **3** White cotton dress, navy-blue spot pattern, bloused bodice, padded shoulders, short puffed sleeves, knot trim, high round neckline bound in plain red, matching pleated belt and mock underskirt, above-knee-length straight skirt. Navy-blue leather shoes, pointed patent-leather toecaps. **4** Black and white checked linen collarless jacket, fitted bodice, edge-to-edge, double loop-and-button fastening, outsized lapels, padded shoulders, inset sleeves, button trim, bias-cut skirts, waterfall at back to above hemline of straight black linen skirt, matching black linen blouse. White leather sling-back shoes, black patent-leather toecaps. **5** Cream linen fitted single-breasted jacket, light-brown pattern, single-button fastening, narrow rounded lapels and collar, matching edges of short skirts and welt pockets, padded shoulders, inset sleeves, button trim. Straight plain cream linen above-knee-length skirt, matching blouse with low sweetheart neckline. Brown leather shoes.

Evening Wear

1 Bright-pink Lycra mini-length dress, fitted and panelled bodice and skirt cut in one piece without waist seam, low off-the-shoulder neckline, draped taffeta stole collar. Black satin shoes, pointed toes, high stiletto heels. **2** Black silk-jersey mini-length dress, wrapover and draped fitted bodice, matching off-the-shoulder neckline, three-quarter-length sleeves and above-knee-length wrapover skirt. Black satin shoes, pointed toes, high stiletto heels. **3** Dark-blue wool and silk two-piece evening suit: double-breasted jacket, long shawl collar faced with dark-blue silk to match covered buttons and piped pockets; tapered trousers, braided outside seams, no turn-ups. White cotton shirt, attached wing collar, concealed fastening. Dark-blue silk bow-tie. Black patent-leather lace-up shoes. **4** Gold lace mini-length dress, fitted bodice, low rounded square neckline bound with gold-coloured satin, matching fitted underdress, full-length unlined inset sleeves, scalloped hems, matching hemline of fitted skirt. Gold kid shoes, pointed toes, high stiletto heels. **5** Royal-blue Lycra strapless mini-length dress, tight skirt and fitted bodice ruched from hemline to under bust, pink lace blouse, collarless neckline bound with pink satin to match hems of full-length inset sleeves, padded shoulders. Royal-blue suede sling-back shoes, high vamps, pointed toes, low heels.

Sports and Leisure Wear

1 Casual wear. Hip-length blue denim jacket, single-breasted button fastening from hipband to under shirt collar, full-length cuffed sleeves, dropped shoulderline, patch pockets under yoke seam, top-stitched edges and detail. Tapered blue denim jeans, side-hip pockets, top-stitched edges and detail. Black knitted-wool cardigan, front-zip fastening. Pale-blue knitted-cotton shirt, small collar, short strap fastening. White trainers. **2** Holiday wear. Fine beige cotton-denim shirt, buttoned collar points, buttoned-strap fastening, full-length sleeves rolled to elbow-level, two breast patch pockets, buttoned flaps, box-pleat detail, narrow shoulder yoke, top-stitched edges and detail. Dark-beige denim tailored knee-length shorts, red leather belt threaded through wide waistband. Dark-blue knitted-cotton sweater, long sleeves tied around hips. Blue canvas lace-up shoes, rubber soles and heels. **3** Beach wear. Multicolour floral patterned cotton knee-length shorts, elasticated waistband. **4** Cycling. Cropped black Lycra top, low scooped neckline, cut-away armholes. Knee-length black Lycra fitted shorts, top-stitched edges. Black leather pumps, round toes, flat heels. **5** Beach wear. Two-piece cotton and Lycra bikini set: mini bra top, small triangular cups, bicolour bright-yellow and royal-blue, narrow rouleau securing band under bust, matching halter straps; briefs with high-cut legs, bright-yellow front panel, royal-blue side panels.

Underwear and Negligee

1 White cotton broderie-anglaise three-piece sleep suit: long edge-to-edge jacket, pointed scalloped front edges which match edges of three-quarter-length flared inset sleeves, hems of self-fabric tie-belt and low neckline of hip-length camisole top, concealed front fastening; full-length trousers flared from knee-level. Green kid slippers, green silk pompon trim. **2** Oyster silk-satin negligee, wrapover front, fastening on side-hip with self-fabric ties, collarless neckline and front edges trimmed with self-colour scalloped-edge lace, matching three-quarter-length trailing sleeves, set into dropped shoulderline, ankle-length flared skirts. **3** Pale-blue satin two-piece underwear set: cropped camisole top, front fastening with self-fabric-covered buttons to under low V-shaped neckline, lace trim, shaping in under bust seams, cut-away armholes; short hipster knickers, flared legs split on curved side seams above hemline. **4** Cream knitted-thermal-cotton two-piece underwear suit, waist-length wrapover top, permanent side fastening above ribbed waist, low neckline piped with cream satin, full-length inset sleeves, ribbed hems, matching ankle-length footless tights. **5** White cotton three-piece lingerie suit, blue and pink butterfly pattern: mini-length wrapover collarless robe, narrow self-fabric tie-belt, short cap sleeves, padded shoulders; strapless bra top, underwired cups, boned front panels, front fastening; short knickers, loop-and-button front fastening.

1989 Day Wear

1 Pink-beige wool two-piece suit: single-breasted jacket, two-button fastening, narrow lapels, edges bound with brown velvet to match hems of full-length inset sleeves, covered buttons and trim on large patch pockets, straight above-knee-length skirt. Brown felt hat, high crown, flat top, brown velvet trim, narrow brim, turned-up edge. Brown leather shoes, pointed toes, stiletto heels. **2** Bright-yellow wool two-piece suit: hip-length wrapover jacket, outsized lapels, padded shoulders, fine yellow-and-black striped yoke, matching cuffs of elbow-length inset sleeves and frilled trim on black patent-leather belt; straight above-knee-length skirt. Yellow felt hat, black half-band at front. Black patent-leather shoes, pointed toecaps. **3** Navy-blue wool double-breasted blazer, dull metal buttons, narrow lapels, flap pockets. Navy-blue and grey checked wool tapered trousers. White cotton collar-attached shirt. Blue and yellow patterned silk tie. Navy-blue leather step-in shoes. **4** Red and white rayon-crepe dress, patterned with flowers, bloused bodice, off-centre fastening, single button under high round neckline, three-quarter-length inset sleeves, gathered on hems and padded shoulders, swathed hip yoke, white and red spotted epaulettes, matching straight above-knee-length skirt. Red leather sling-back shoes, thick straps, pointed toes, low heels. **5** Egg-yellow wool edge-to-edge coat, narrow lapels, collar worn turned up, padded shoulders, full-length cuffed sleeves, seamed at short sleeve-level, large patch pockets, wide black suede buckled belt. Black knitted-wool polo-neck sweater-dress, straight above-knee-length skirt. Black felt hat, wide turned-back brim. Black suede gloves. Black knitted-wool tights. Black suede shoes.

Evening Wear

1 Black silk and wool two-piece evening suit: edge-to-edge hip-length semi-fitted jacket, fastening from curved hem to under high round neckline with loops and buttons, gold braid edging, matching hems of full-length inset sleeves, padded shoulders, either side centre-front and hems of jacket and sleeves embroidered with fine gold russian braid, beads and sequins in a paisley-style pattern; straight ankle-length skirt, back split. Black satin shoes, pointed toes. **2** Black silk-jersey evening dress, fitted bodice and ankle-length skirt cut in one piece without waist seam, fitted bra top, cups embroidered with tiny silver beads and sequins, fine self-jersey rouleau shoulder straps. Black satin shoes, pointed toes, tapered heels. **3** Pink, red and gold patterned silk cocktail dress, hip-length fitted boned strapless bodice, straight across neckline, straight above-knee-length skirt, trimmed with swirls of accordion-pleated self-fabric. Red satin shoes, pointed toes. **4** Gold lamé evening dress, fitted bodice ruched from hip-level to under bustline, upper bodice draped over bust from padded shoulders, forming low square neckline, full-length inset sleeves, ground-length pleated skirt. Gold sequined clutch bag; gold kid shoes, pointed toes. **5** Red leather top and skirt, fitted and boned corset-style bodice, low hip-level centre point, seamed bra top, narrow shoulder straps, straight mini-length skirt. Black velvet shoes, two laced bar straps, pointed toes, high stiletto heels.

Sports and Leisure Wear

1 Holiday wear. Pink Lycra top, front midriff open from side to high-centre-front point under bust, drapery from point of low V-shaped neckline, low-cut and cut-away armholes, top-stitched edges. Pink and yellow patterned harem trousers, full legs gathered from low hip yoke seam, elasticated hems, narrow waistband. Pink leather mules, open toes, flat heels. **2** Exercise wear. Stretch-Lycra all-in-one bodysuit, low scooped neckline edged in yellow, matching hip-length side-hip panels, orange bust-level yoke and short sleeves, lime-green body and legs, edges and seams outlined in black, top-stitched hems. **3** Beach wear. Ice-blue shiny stretch-Lycra swimsuit, waist-length wrapover V-shaped neckline formed between pleated halter straps, low back, high-cut legs. **4** Casual wear. Red and white striped cotton shirt, pointed collar, worn open, buttoned-strap fastening, two large breast patch pockets, buttoned flaps, narrow shoulder yoke, full-length sleeves worn rolled to elbow-level. White polyester-cotton tapered trousers, side-hip pockets, pleats from waistband, blue leather belt. Red leather step-in shoes, mock lace-up fastenings, white man-made soles and heels. **5** Cycling. Green cotton top, wrapover front, side-waist tie, notched roll collar, padded shoulders, cap sleeves. Mini-length red cotton divided skirt, gathers from under narrow hip yoke, flared legs, top-stitched edges. Blue leather step-in shoes, high tongues, round toes, flat heels.

Accessories

1 Natural straw hat, high crown, curled brim. **2** White canvas shoes, open fronts and toes, white and red spotted straps and bow trim. **3** White silk hat, draped crown, self-fabric bow trim, wide brim. **4** Black leather shoulder bag, gilt trim, long handle. **5** Brown felt hat, large crown, wide brim. Fake-fur collar. **6** Black felt hat, tall crown, russian braid trim, straight brim. Black and red patterned polyester scarf. **7** Navy-blue leather sling-back shoes, flat heels. **8** White leather shoes, brown toecaps, trim and high louis heels. **9** Tan leather bag, flap, concealed fastening, saddle-stitched trim, short handle. **10** Green felt hat, tall crown, flat top, wide brim. Green silk scarf. **11** White straw hat, large crown, turned-up outsized brim trimmed in brown. **12** Dark-blue drawstring bag, gilt trim, long handle. **13** Natural straw hat, pointed crown, turned-up brim, blue and brown striped trim. **14** Cream shoes, sage-green snakeskin cross-over straps. **15** Brimless mock-leopard-skin hat, ruched crown; matching fur earrings. **16** Black fur hat, large crown covered in ostrich feather spikes, wide brim. **17** Mock-leopard-skin pumps, flat heels. **18** Mock-snakeskin elastic-sided boots, pointed toes, flared heels. **19** Mock-tiger-skin shoes, pointed toes, strap-and-buckle fastening. **20** Brown felt hat, large crown, fake-fur trim. **21** Brown and cream two-tone shoes, laced through metal rings. **22** Tan leather shoes, almond-shaped toes, strap-and-buckle fastenings. **23** Olive-green lace-up shoes, decorative self-leather thonging, top-stitched detail.

Chart of the Development of 1980s Fashion

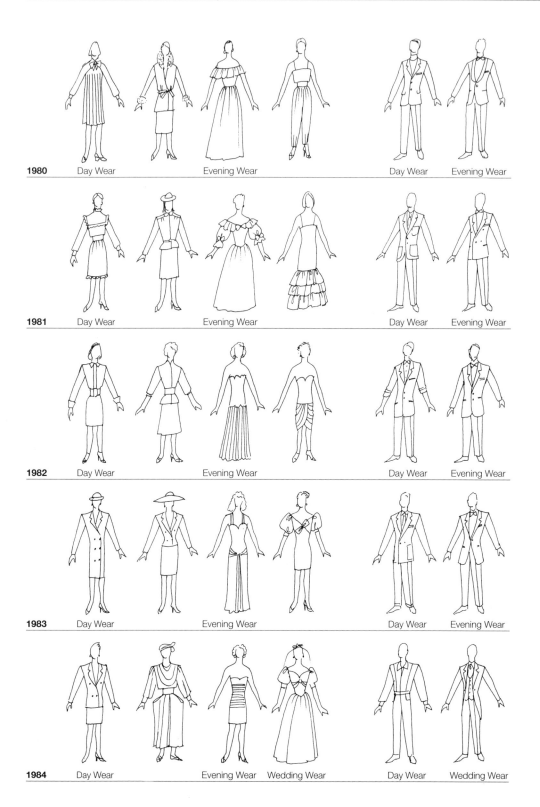

1980 Day Wear	Evening Wear	Day Wear — Evening Wear
1981 Day Wear	Evening Wear	Day Wear — Evening Wear
1982 Day Wear	Evening Wear	Day Wear — Evening Wear
1983 Day Wear	Evening Wear	Day Wear — Evening Wear
1984 Day Wear	Evening Wear Wedding Wear	Day Wear — Wedding Wear

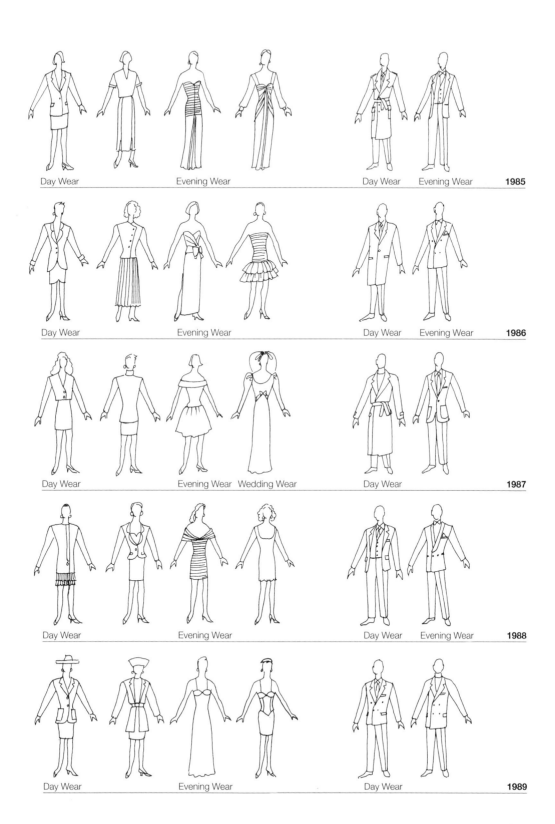

Day Wear   Evening Wear   Day Wear   Evening Wear   **1985**

Day Wear   Evening Wear   Day Wear   Evening Wear   **1986**

Day Wear   Evening Wear Wedding Wear   Day Wear   **1987**

Day Wear   Evening Wear   Day Wear   Evening Wear   **1988**

Day Wear   Evening Wear   Day Wear   **1989**

Biographies of Designers

Alaïa, Azzedine 1940–. Designer. Born Tunisia. Alaïa studied at the Ecole des Beaux-Arts in Tunis before moving in 1957 to Paris where he worked for Dior, Laroche and Mugler. During the 1970s he designed for private clients, launching his first collection in 1981. A revolutionary design for a black leather tunic brought him international recognition. He sought in his designs to enhance the female silhouette, experimenting with flexible fabrics such as wool, leather and Lycra, to create complex garments that clung to the body like a second skin. He popularized the stretch look and made practical yet sexy use of the zipper.

Armani, Giorgio 1935–. Designer. Born Piacenza, Italy. Armani worked from 1954 to 1960 as a window stylist, and eventually as fashion coordinator, for the Italian department store La Rinascente. He designed menswear for Cerruti from 1970 until 1974, when he turned freelance. He opened his own company in 1975. Known for his simple, precise tailoring and for the uncluttered, minimalist look of his clothes, Armani was particularly influential among working women in the late 1970s and 1980s when he contributed wide shoulders to the 'power suit' popular at that time. By the mid-1980s his designs were sleeker and less pronounced. He created large, loose blazers and supple shorts and culottes, invariably in muted tones.

Beene, Geoffrey 1927–. Designer. Born Haynesville, Louisiana, USA. Beene studied at the Traphagen School of Fashion in New York. In the late 1940s he moved to Paris where he trained at the Académie Julian and at Maison Molyneux. On his return to New York in 1948, he worked for a number of ready-to-wear companies before founding his own firm in 1963. A master of cut, Beene combines the quality of couture with the ease of modern sportswear. He is known for blending rich fabrics with less expensive materials.

Blahnik, Manolo 1943–. Shoe designer. Born Santa Cruz, Canary Islands. Blahnik studied literature at the University of Geneva until 1968 when he moved to Paris to study art for a year at the Ecole du Louvre. In 1971 he went to New York where

his portfolio aroused the interest of US fashion editors who encouraged him in the production of his first shoe collection that same year. Blahnik moved to London in 1971 and in 1973 opened 'Zapata', his first shop. He combines hand-craftsmanship with modern techniques, employing a wide range of materials and vivid colours with equal flair to create ethereal footwear which blends elegance and fantasy.

Body Map Designer label. David Holah 1958–. Born London, England. Stevie Stewart 1958–. Born London, England. Both designers studied at Middlesex Polytechnic until 1982, when they formed the company Body Map in London. One of the brightest design teams of the 1980s, they produced innovative, witty garments which were loose and layered, predominantly in black, white or cream.

Comme des Garçons *See* **Kawakubo, Rei**

Conran, Jasper 1959–. Designer. Born London, England. Conran attended Parsons School of Art and Design in New York until 1977, when he worked for a short time as a designer at Fiorucci. He then returned to London and created a womenswear collection for Henri Bendel, the New York department store. In 1977 he worked as a consultant for the British firm Wallis before launching his first collection the following year. His basic style has remained constant – a practical simplicity of design using quality fabrics to produce a comfortable and easy fit.

Ellis, Perry 1940–86. Designer. Born Portsmouth, Virginia, USA. Ellis completed a BA in business studies at the College of William and Mary in Williamsburg, Virginia, and an MA in retailing at New York University, graduating in 1963. He worked until 1967 as a sportswear buyer for Miller & Rhoads department store in Richmond, Virginia, before becoming design director for John Meyer of Norwich, New York, and, in 1974, sportswear designer for the Vera companies, where he was given his own label. He started his own company in 1980. Ellis's clothes had the casual ease of sportswear and captured the essence of the American look.

His womenswear was playful yet graceful – smart coats and trousers, often cut on mannish lines.

Galliano, John (Charles) 1960–. Designer. Born Gibraltar. Galliano trained at St Martin's School of Art in London, graduating in 1984 with a highly acclaimed final-year collection inspired by the French Revolution. Part of a new breed of avant-garde British designers which emerged in the 1980s, he has dedicated himself to pushing fashion forward by learning from the past. His innovative and exciting designs are historically influenced, yet highly contemporary. A diverse mixture of cultures and epochs, materials and colours combine in his clothes to produce an entirely new look.

Gaultier, Jean-Paul 1952–. Designer. Born Paris, France. At the age of seventeen Gaultier sent sketches to several couture houses and in 1970 was invited to work for Cardin for one year. He then designed for Jacques Esterel and Jean Patou, among others. In 1977 he set up his own company, producing witty, anarchic fashions which revamped Parisian couture by injecting fleamarket kitsch and London streetstyle. He has developed a reputation for challenging accepted gender boundaries.

Gigli, Romeo 1950–. Designer. Born Bologna, Italy. Gigli studied architecture. He challenged the tailored traditions of Italian fashion with his first collection in 1984, a bohemian array of long, languorous dresses in sober colours. Integral to his designs is a classicism that lends a subtlety and balance to each garment. In the 1980s his collections were based on dance clothes – stretch fabrics were shaped to create a body-skimming purity of cut.

Hamnett, Katharine 1948–. Designer. Born Gravesend, Kent, England. Hamnett attended St Martin's School of Art in London, graduating in 1969. She worked freelance for European and Japanese firms until she set up her own company in 1979. For early collections she produced functional garments based on traditional workwear. In the 1980s she became famous for her 'Choose Life' T-shirt collection – T-shirts printed with political and

environmental slogans. In 1986, she produced a 'power dressing' collection which epitomized eighties style.

Jones, Stephen 1957–. Milliner. Born West Kirby, Liverpool, England. Jones trained at High Wycombe School of Art in Buckinghamshire until 1976 and St Martin's School of Art in London until 1979. After working briefly at Lachasse, he opened his own business in 1980. His quirky, asymmetric designs reintroduced millinery to the fashion world.

Kamali, Norma (Arraez) 1945–. Designer. Born New York, USA. Kamali studied fashion illustration at the Fashion Institute of Technology in New York. Between 1967 and 1978 she worked as a freelance designer, opening a boutique with her husband in 1968. In the 1970s she produced extrovert, body-conscious clothes such as hot pants, gold lamé maillots and high-cut bikinis – beach fashions that became increasingly popular in the 1980s. In 1978, after her divorce, she set up the company OMO (On My Own) and in 1981 introduced her famous 'sweats', a line in sweatshirt fleece fabric for daywear, including the 'rah-rah skirt', which proved phenomenally successful.

Karan, Donna (Faske) 1948–. Designer. Born Forest Hills, New York. Karan trained at Parsons School of Design in New York and during her second year worked as a sketcher at Anne Klein where, after graduating, she spent almost a year before moving to Addenda. In 1968 she returned to Anne Klein and in 1969 took over from Klein, becoming co-designer for the company with Louis Dell'Olio. In 1984 she set up her own label, DKNY, which has expanded to produce accessories, beauty products and perfume as well as clothes. From the sportswear that she designed for Anne Klein to the practical stretch fabric bodysuits and bodywraps for which she is known, her aim has been to create sexy and wearable clothes for the modern woman.

Kawakubo, Rei 1942–. Designer. Born Tokyo, Japan. Kawakubo studied literature at Keio University in Tokyo. After graduating in 1964, she worked at Asahi Kasei, a Japanese textile company. In 1966 she turned freelance and introduced the Comme des Garçons label in 1969. She became famous in the late 1970s/early 1980s for her radical redefinition of womenswear. Her androgynous designs, incorporating tears, knots and slashes in unexpected places, deconstructed the conventional female silhouette. Though sombre and sexless, her clothes had a great influence on fashion in the 1980s.

Klein, Calvin (Richard) 1942–. Designer. Born New York, USA. After studying at the New York Fashion Institute of Technology, Klein joined Dan Millstein in 1962 and then worked freelance until 1968 when he set up Calvin Klein Co. He became famous for his sleek, understated suits and sportswear made from natural fabrics. The late 1970s witnessed the hugely successful marketing of his 'designer label' jeans and in the 1980s his notorious advertisements for men's and women's underwear and for fragrances made him a household name worldwide.

Lacroix, Christian 1951–. Designer. Born Arles, France. Lacroix attended the Sorbonne in Paris where in 1976 he completed a course in museum studies. From 1978 to 1980 he worked with Paulin at Hermès and in 1981 became artistic director at Patou. In 1987 he opened his own couture and ready-to-wear house in Paris. Lacroix creates bold designs: exotic and unusual combinations of luxurious materials and vivid colours, influenced by his frequent forays to museums and markets as well as by the Provence of his childhood. He has reintroduced such fashion staples as the frou-frou petticoat and puffball skirt, and has revitalized couture as a source of inspiration for the ready-to-wear industry.

Lagerfeld, Karl (Otto) 1938–. Designer. Born Hamburg, Germany. Lagerfeld was employed by Balmain at the age of seventeen after winning a design competition sponsored by the International Wool Secretariat. In 1958 he became art director at Patou and one year later began to work freelance for several design houses, including Chloé, Krizia and Fendi. Lagerfeld made a considerable impact on 1970s fashions with his innovative ideas, two of which were to dye furs in

vibrant colours and to remove the linings from fur coats, making them more supple and lightweight. At Chloé he became renowned for feminine eveningwear of the highest quality. From 1983, as design director of Chanel, he combined the company's hallmark tweed suits and gilt buttons with modern, streetstyle elements to create the characteristic blend of stylishness and impudence that has informed all his work.

Lauren, Ralph 1939–. Designer. Born New York, USA. While studying business at City College in New York, Lauren worked for Bloomingdales and Brooks Brothers, among others. Appointed designer for Beau Brummell Neckwear in 1967, he created 'Polo', a line of luxury handmade ties. In 1968 he began designing menswear for the Polo division. Womenswear was added in 1971. In 1972 he launched his own label, employing high-quality tweeds and fine cotton to create an elegant look redolent of F. Scott Fitzgerald's America. He incorporated other facets of America's past into his 'prairie look' of 1978, based on fringed leather jackets, full-sleeved cotton blouses and denim skirts worn over white petticoats, and into his 'frontier fashion' of the 1980s, with its hooded capes and ruffled blouses. His work is informed by the belief that fashion should be timeless.

Missoni, Ottavio and Rosita Knitwear designers. Ottavio 1921–. Born Dalmatia, Yugoslavia. Rosita 1931–. Born Lombardy, Italy. After founding the Missoni company in 1953, the couple produced their first knitwear collection for the Rinascente stores in 1954 and launched their own label in 1958. They rose to prominence in the 1970s, producing fluid, boldly patterned dresses, coats and sweaters which restored the fashion world's interest in knitwear. Missoni is known for sophisticated knitting techniques and an artistic blending of colour. Both modern and classic, their designs became status symbols in the 1970s and 1980s.

Miyake, Issey 1938–. Designer. Born Hiroshima, Japan. Miyake graduated in 1964 from Tama University in Tokyo. In 1965 he moved to Paris to study at the Ecole de la Chambre Syndicale

de la Haute Couture. He then worked for Laroche and Givenchy before joining Geoffrey Beene in New York in 1969. He founded the Miyake Design Studio in 1970 and showed his first collection in New York in 1971. An experimental and visionary artist, he creates highly original garments, many of which can be draped around the body in different ways. Using traditional Japanese techniques of layering fabric, he explores texture and structure with unusual materials such as moulded plastic and woven bamboo.

Montana, Claude 1949–. Designer. Born Paris, France. Montana began his career selling handmade papier-mâché jewelry decorated with rhinestones in London street-markets. His designs appeared in British *Vogue*. When he returned to Paris in 1972 he worked for MacDouglas and Complice, founding his own house in 1979. He produces tough, masculine garments, often in leather. The Montana aesthetic of designing assertive women's clothing without sacrificing the female form contributed to the evolution of the power look of the mid-1980s.

Moschino, Franco 1950–94. Designer. Born Abbiategrasso, Italy. Moschino studied fine art at the Accademia di Belle Arti in Milan from 1967 to 1969, then worked as an illustrator on various magazines. From 1972 to 1977 he was an illustrator for Versace. After designing eleven collections for Cadette, he opened his own company in 1983. Moschino combined basic shapes and traditional methods with irreverent, ironic, often surrealistic imagery to create clothes designed to poke fun at the fashion industry – a black mini skirt hemmed with plastic fried eggs, for example.

Mugler, Thierry 1948–. Designer. Born Strasbourg, France. In 1966 Mugler joined Gudule boutique in Paris as assistant designer. In 1973 he created a collection under the label 'Café de Paris' and set up his own house in 1974. Strongly influenced by Hollywood glamour as well as science fiction and sexual fetishism, he produces clinging, theatrical clothes which can either be highly minimalist or vampy and ornate. In 1977 he was one of the first designers to

use padded shoulders and in the 1980s he employed these, along with tight skirts and armour-like corsetry, to create a look that exuded sexual power.

Ozbek, Rifat 1954–. Designer. Born Istanbul, Turkey. Ozbek moved to England in 1970. He studied architecture at Liverpool University, followed by fashion design at St Martin's School of Art, graduating in 1977. In 1978 he worked with Walter Albini for Trell, Milan, and in 1980 became a designer for Monsoon, London. In 1984 he established his own company. In a luxurious combination of ethnicity and London streetstyle, he embellishes the classic shapes of Western couture with decorative references to other cultures. He was best known in the mid-1980s for his richly embroidered black cocktail suits and, later in the decade, for his sarong skirts, midriff tops and hipster trousers.

Rabanne, Paco 1934–. Designer. Born San Sebastian, Spain. Rabanne's mother was chief seamstress at Balenciaga in Spain. His family moved to France during the Spanish Civil War and Rabanne studied architecture at the Ecole des Beaux-Arts, Paris, graduating in 1964. He started his career designing plastic jewelry and buttons for Balenciaga, Dior and Givenchy. In 1965 he applied his experience in plastics to dressmaking, and continued to experiment with the use of innovative fabrics. Preferring the title of engineer to that of couturier, he makes dresses out of metal discs, chains, paper – even aluminium. He frequently designs costumes for cinema, theatre and ballet.

Saint Laurent, Yves (Henri Donat Mathieu) 1936–. Designer. Born Oran, Algeria. In 1954 Saint Laurent won first prize for a cocktail dress design in a competition held by the International Wool Secretariat. In 1955 he began working for Dior, taking over the house at the age of twenty-one when Dior died. Though hugely popular, his youthful style did not please Dior's more conventional clientele and in 1961 he was replaced by Marc Bohan. The following year he established his own house and in 1966 introduced his ready-to-wear line, Rive Gauche. Famous for his feminizing of the male wardrobe, he has produced many of the sophisticated and innovative classics of post-war women's style, including his influential 'smoking' jackets, see-through blouses, shirt dresses and safari jackets. His collections in the late 1970s and 1980s, showing full skirts, harem trousers and tunics in vivid colours, brought ethnic dressing to haute couture.

Smith, Paul 1946–. Designer. Born Nottingham, England. Smith started his career at eighteen, working in a clothing warehouse. In 1970 he opened in Nottingham one of the first shops outside London to stock designer clothing. He then took evening courses and began designing his own clothes. In 1976 he became consultant to an Italian manufacturer and to the International Wool Secretariat, and launched the Paul Smith label later the same year. In 1979 he opened his first London shop. His simple, stylish clothes in offbeat patterns and colours for both men and women are widely popular. In the 1980s he was responsible for the revival of boxer shorts and the Filofax.

Ungaro, Emanuel (Matteolti) 1933–. Designer. Born Aix-en-Provence, France, to Italian parents. Ungaro trained in his parents' tailoring firm and then moved to Paris in 1955. He worked for Maison Camps until he joined Balenciaga in 1958, and in 1963 he moved to Courrèges. Three years later he founded his own house, producing such futuristic designs as angular coats, thigh-high boots and metal bras. In the 1970s and 1980s his clothes became more supple. Ungaro often experiments with rich, boldly printed materials and contrasting textures to create majestic, billowing garments influenced by his mentor, Balenciaga.

Versace, Gianni 1946–97. Designer. Born Calabria, Italy. Versace worked with his dressmaker mother before moving to Milan in 1972 where he worked freelance for Genny, Complice and Callaghan. During the 1970s he developed a reputation for eveningwear, leatherwear and leather-trimmed knitwear. In 1978 he founded his

own company. Versace designed sensuous, clinging garments, often cut on the bias. He explored the use of different textures and patterns, introducing a lightweight aluminium-mesh cloth in 1982. His collections were bold, sexy and modern, and combined classical craftsmanship with innovative experimentation. After his death, his sister, Donatella, took over as designer.

Westwood, Vivienne (Swire) 1941–. Designer. Born Derbyshire, England. Westwood attended Harrow Art School for one term, leaving to become a teacher. In 1971 she began designing for the shop that she opened in Chelsea with Malcolm McLaren, variously known as 'Let it Rock', 'Too Fast to Live, Too Young to Die', 'Sex', 'Seditionaries' and 'World's End'. In 1981 she presented the Pirate collection, her first London catwalk show, and in 1983 began to show in Paris, gaining a worldwide reputation. The following year her partnership with McLaren came to an end. Anarchic subversion is integral

to her work, from the fetishistic Bondage collection inspired by her association with the punk subculture of the 1970s, to the sexually loaded reinvention of the Victorian crinoline in 'Mini-crini', her collection for Spring/Summer 1985. Westwood continually plunders ideas from other cultures, both past and present, and twists them into rebellion.

Yamamoto, Yohji 1943–. Designer. Born Tokyo, Japan. Yamamoto studied law at Keio University. He graduated in 1966, then attended Bunka College of Fashion, Tokyo, until 1969, when he became a freelance designer. He set up his own company in 1972 and in 1977 launched his first collection in Japan. Guided by the Japanese philosophy that irregular forms are beautiful in their lack of artifice, Yamamoto, like his contemporaries Kawakubo and Miyake, rejects the conventional female fashion silhouette, creating sombre, unstructured garments that layer and drape the body. They often have oddly placed flaps and lopsided hems.

Sources for 1980s Fashion

Cardin, Pierre
Pierre Cardin: Past, Present and Future, 1990

Carnegy, Vicky
Fashions of a Decade: The 1980s, 1990

Chenoune, Farid
A History of Men's Fashion, 1993

De Courtais, Georgina
Women's Headdress and Hairstyles, 1973

De la Haye, Amy
The Cutting Edge: 50 Years of British Fashion 1947–1997, 1996

De Marly, Diana
Fashion for Men: An Illustrated History, 1985

Ewing, Elizabeth
Fur in Dress, 1981

Kennett, Frances
The Collectors' Book of Twentieth Century Fashion, 1983

Laver, James
and Amy de la Haye
Costume and Fashion: A Concise History, 1995

Lee-Potter, Charlie
Sportswear in Vogue Since 1910, 1984

Martin, Richard
and Harold Koda
Jocks and Nerds: Men's Style in the Twentieth Century, 1989

Miyake, Issey
Issey Miyake: Photographs by Irving Penn, 1988

Mulvagh, Jane
Vogue: History of 20th Century Fashion, 1988

O'Hara, Georgina
The Encyclopaedia of Fashion, 1986

Peacock, John
Costume 1066 to the 1990s, 1994
The Chronicle of Western Costume, 1991
20th Century Fashion, 1993
Men's Fashion, 1996

Polhemus, Ted
Street Style, 1994

Pedro, Simon
The Bikini, 1986

Ribeiro, Aileen
Dress and Morality, 1986

Robinson, Julian
The Fine Art of Fashion: An Illustrated History, 1989

Ginsburg, Madeleine
The Hat: Trends and Traditions, 1990

Magazines
Donna, Milan

Elle, London

For Him, London

GQ, Gentleman's Quarterly, New York

Harpers & Queen (Harpers & Queen International), London

Harrods Magazine, London 1985–1987

L'Officiel de la couture et de la mode de Paris, Paris

L'Uomo Vogue, Milan

Per Lui, Milan

Sposabella, Milan

Vogue, New York

Vogue, London

Vogue, Paris

Vogue Italia, Milan

Vogue Patterns, New York

Vogue Patterns, London

Catalogues
Ciao Sportswear, London, Spring/Summer 1985

Costume Changes: Jewellery Department, 1987

Harrods, Grosvenor Fur Collection, London, 1982–1985

International Menswear Fair Catalogue, 1984

Lingerie Luxury: Lingerie Collection, 1987

Martinique Club Adventure, London, 1988

Marc O'Polo, London, Spring/Summer 1985

Relay: Menswear, Summer 1985